CHICAGO

THOMAS AND VIRGINIA AYLESWORTH

GREAT
CITIES

A BLACKBIRCH PRESS™ BOOK

THE ROSEN PUBLISHING GROUP, INC.

Published by Blackbirch Press™ in conjunction with The Rosen Publishing Group, Inc.
29 East 21st Street, New York, NY 10010

©1990 Blackbirch Press™ a division of Blackbirch Graphics, Inc.
First Edition

Printed in Hong Kong
Bound in the United States of America

Editors: Kailyard Associates
Editorial Assistant: Norma L. Ginsberg
Art Director: Cynthia Minichino
Maps: Robert Italiano

Library of Congress Cataloging-in-Publication Data

Aylesworth, Thomas G.
  Chicago / Thomas and Virginia Aylesworth.
  (Great cities)
  Includes bibliographical references and index.
  Summary: Describes the city of Chicago, its history and people.
  1. Chicago (Ill.)—History—Juvenile literature. 2. Chicago
(Ill.)—Description—1981- —Guide-books—Juvenile literature.
[(1. Chicago (Ill.)] I. Aylesworth, Virginia L. II. Title. III. Series.
F548.33.A95 1990   90-38245
977.3'11—dc20   CIP
ISBN 0-8239-1209-4   AC

(Pages 4-5)
Lake Shore Drive winds north along Lake Michigan, where high-rises border Lincoln Park.

CONTENTS

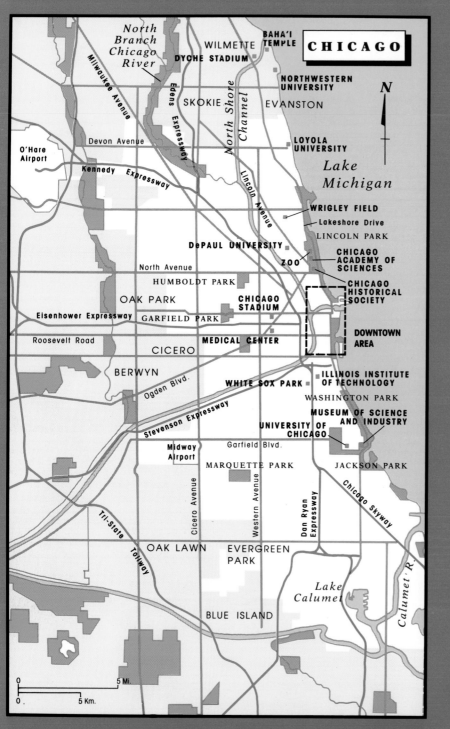

"Chicago, Chicago, that toddlin' town."
Fred Fisher—songwriter

Population: 3,009,530. Chicago, the nation's third most populous city, has a population density of 13,180 people per square mile. People over 65 make up 11.4 percent of the population, and 58.5 percent of the people in Chicago are under 35 years of age. Whites number 1,512,411, and blacks number 1,197,174. Other large ethnic populations are Indians, Eskimos, and Aleuts (6802); Asians and Pacific Islanders (73,745); and Hispanics (423,357). Foreign-born residents make up 10.5 percent of the city's population.

Size: The city covers 228 square miles.

Nickname: "The Windy City" is Chicago's nickname, although 11 prominent cities in the nation have higher average wind velocities. Real Chicagoans never call their town "Chi."

Motto: "I Will" is the unofficial motto of Chicago.

Main Businesses: Chicago is the nation's second largest industrial center, and among the manufactured goods produced there are steel and iron, food products, machinery, fabricated metal products, chemicals, transportation equipment, and petroleum products. Printing and publishing are also important industries, and there are many research laboratories in the city. In trade businesses, Chicago is

Chicago-O'Hare International Airport, the busiest in the United States.

the nation's leading wholesale distribution center, and the grain market and farm products center of the country. The city is the financial capital of the Midwest, the world's busiest railroad and airline center, and a leading world port.

Communication: Chicago has nine television stations and 31 radio stations. The two main newspapers are the *Chicago Tribune* (circulation 740,154—seventh in the nation) and the *Chicago Sun-Times* (circulation 554,670—twelfth in the nation).

Education: There are over 700 elementary schools and more than 60 high schools, both public and private, in the city. In addition, there are 95 institutions of higher education in Chicago. The Chicago Public Library, with its 55 branches, contains millions of volumes.

City Seal: Around the edge of the circular seal is inscribed "City of Chicago—Incorporated 4th March 1837." A shield with stars and stripes is in the center, as are a native American, a sailing ship, and a sheaf of wheat, symbolizing the city's national character, the city's first residents, the coming of commerce, and activity and piety, respectively. Also included are a baby in a pearl shell, symbolizing the city's future as "the gem of the ocean," and the Latin words *Urbs in Horto*, which mean "City in a Garden."

City Flag: Chicago's flag has four red stars and two blue stripes on a white background. The stars symbolize the building of Fort Dearborn, the Chicago Fire, and the city's two world's fairs. The stripes represent the two branches of the Chicago River.

(At left)
Wildflowers grow abundantly in the midst of skyscrapers.

THE PLACE

"I have struck a city—a real city— and they call it Chicago."

Rudyard Kipling—British writer, on a tour of the United States

Fireworks light up the Chicago skyline.

Chicago is located in the northwestern corner of Illinois on Lake Michigan—a true "inland sea" that is five times larger than the whole state of Connecticut.

The city lies on a flat plain that averages 595 feet above sea level and features cold winters and hot summers. Flowing west from Lake Michigan through the center of the city is the Chicago River, which has been called "the river that flows backward." The river flowed eastward into the lake until 1900, when sewage from the river began to pollute Lake Michigan. As the city has always taken its drinking water from the lake, engineers reversed the river's flow.

West of Lake Michigan about a mile, the Chicago River divides into two branches, forming a "Y." Mainly because of this, the city is divided into four major sections. Downtown Chicago, which includes Grant Park on the lake and the famous business district called "the Loop," lies just south of the Chicago River. The North Side is located north of the river; the West Side extends to the west of the two river branches; and the South Side includes all of the city south of the downtown section.

Chicago's streets are laid out in a grid pattern, with occasional diagonal-running streets. State and Madison streets are the baselines of the city's street numbering system. State Street runs north and south, dividing Chicago into east and west numbers. Madison Street, which runs east and west, divides the city into north and south numbers.

(At right)
Lake Michigan is a favorite spot for sailboats in the summer.

Stretching along the lakefront, Grant Park has been the place to play and relax for generations of Chicagoans.

The city has about 26 miles of lakefront, and along the lake is a superb chain of parks and parkways, with Chicago's tallest and finest buildings rising behind them. Even with its towering skyscrapers, Chicago never gives the feeling that is so common in other cities—the hemmed-in feeling—the feeling that the buildings will fall at any minute—the feeling that the sun will never shine on the street. The streets and avenues are so wide, the sidewalks so spacious, that the feeling is almost like walking on a broad boulevard between monuments.

Trains rumble through the downtown district on tracks built above the streets.

Michigan Avenue is undoubtedly the showcase of the downtown area. Near the Loop—the business core of Chicago, so-called because it is ringed by the elevated railroad tracks—it is a wide street with magnificent old buildings on the west, and, except for a few fine buildings, the beautiful expanse of Grant Park on the east. Going north on Michigan Avenue, after one passes the Chicago River, it is the Magnificent Mile, containing some of the finest and largest stores in the country, as well as elegant hotels and office buildings.

Near the north end of the Magnificent Mile is the Water Tower, at the corner of Michigan and Chicago avenues. This was one of the few buildings to survive the Chicago Fire of 1871. Grant Park stands between Michigan Avenue and the lake, and the park is truly Chicago's beautiful "front yard."

What sticks in the mind is its beauty—the famous skyline, the 131 forest preserves, the 572 city parks, the 35 museums, and the 31 beaches.

(*At left*)
First Chicago Clock at First Plaza.

THE PAST

"Hog butcher for the world,
Tool maker, stacker of wheat,
Player with railroads and the nation's
* freight handler,*
Stormy, husky, brawling,
City of the big shoulders."

Carl Sandburg —American poet
and biographer

Entrance to the Art Institute of Chicago.

Chicago has always been a transportation center. Long before the arrival of European settlers, the area was important to the Indians, who used it as an overland route, or portage, from the Des Plaines River to the Chicago River, where they then paddled their canoes to Lake Michigan. Not many of them actually lived in the area, because the land on both sides of the Chicago River was low and wet—mostly bog land. And what is now the Loop was only a few inches higher than the lake and, consequently, was under water for several months of the year.

The river itself was filled with wild rice, except for a narrow channel, and on the banks were huge beds of skunk cabbage and wild onion—home to large numbers of skunks. Still, because of the portage, it was a meeting place for Indians on their way to hunt or make war.

It is probable that two Frenchmen, Father Jacques Marquette and Louis Joliet, were the first Europeans to set foot in the area that was to become Chicago. In 1673, they followed the portage on their way to the future Green Bay, Wisconsin. During the winter of 1674–1675, Father Marquette returned with two companions, and they camped near the Chicago River.

The first real settler, however, was a black man— Jean Baptiste Point du Sable—a French-speaking businessman who opened a trading post on the north bank of the river in 1779. He married a Pottowatomie woman, learned the language, and lived peacefully

Wolf Point in 1833, an overland route for Indians on their way to Lake Michigan.

Fort Dearborn was home to a company of U.S. soldiers from 1804–1812, during which time it became an important trading post.

among the native Americans for many years. In 1800, he sold his establishment and moved to St. Charles, Missouri.

In 1787, when the Northwest Territory was created by Congress, the area became a part of the United States. Even so, the native Americans controlled the area until 1794, when they were defeated by General "Mad Anthony" Wayne in the Battle of Fallen Timbers, near what is now Toledo, Ohio. As a result of the battle, the new nation was given "one piece of land Six Miles Square at the mouth of the Chicakgo River."

There is an argument about what "Chicakgo," or more correctly, "Checagou," meant. No one doubts that it was an Indian word, but some historians say that it meant "skunk," or "wild onion," both of which are still fairly common in the area. Others think it meant "big," "great," or "powerful."

Life was still hazardous in the Northwest Territory, and in 1803, a company of United States soldiers arrived in the area that would become Chicago. Under the command of Captain John Whistler, they were to build a fort to protect the territory. Fort Dearborn was completed in 1804, near the present-day intersection of Wacker Drive and Michigan Avenue. Within eight years there was a small settlement near the fort, which had become an important trading center. But by then the War of 1812 had begun, and the federal government, feeling that Fort Dearborn could not be defended, ordered the troops to abandon it.

Wild onion

So, on August 15, 1812, 97 soldiers and settlers left the fort. They were soon attacked by Indians in the pay of the British Army, and more than half of them were killed. The rest were captured, and the fort was burned.

It wasn't until 1816, when the army rebuilt the fort, that settlers began to move back into the area. By 1818 a settlement had once again been established near the fort, and this village became part of the new state of Illinois. Still, it took until 1830 for the citizens to establish town boundaries. That year a commission proposed a canal to be built, extending from the town of Ottawa, to the west, to Chicago, and both towns were laid out.

In 1833 Chicago was incorporated as a town, even though it had been the county seat of Cook County since 1831. Finally, on March 4, 1837, Chicago was incorporated as a city, even though it had a population of only 4000.

In 1848 the Illinois and Michigan Canal was completed, and Chicago's future was assured. The canal, running from La Salle, Illinois, to Chicago, became a major waterway for farmers to the west to get their products to Chicago, and from there to the eastern markets via the Great Lakes. When the canal opened, Chicago had a population of 20,000. But then it became a major shipping center, and in two years the population had zoomed to 30,000.

Chicago was on its way to becoming the nation's transportation center in 1848, when the Galena and

(*At right*)
The Union Stockyards were formed in 1865 and made Chicago the meat packing center of the country.

ICE POND

TRANSIT PARK

The National Union Republican Convention at Crosby's Opera House, where Abraham Lincoln was nominated for President.

Chicago Union Railroad, the city's first railroad, began its operations. The Illinois Central Railroad began operating in 1856, and by 1860, Chicago had become the largest city in Illinois, with 112,172 people. It was in that year, 1860, that Chicago hosted its first national presidential convention, when Abraham Lincoln was nominated for the nation's highest office by the Republican party.

Although huge numbers of Chicago men and boys left to fight in the Civil War, Chicago prospered between 1861 and 1865. Cattle poured into the city's stockyards and, with the formation of the Union Stockyards at 43rd and Halsted streets in 1865, the city became a leader in the nation's meat packing industry. It has been said that the North won the Civil War as much because of the meat flowing out of Chicago to the Union Army as their proficiency on the battlefield. The grain trade also boomed, and the Chicago Board of Trade became the chief grain market in the country. Cyrus Hall McCormick, the inventor of the farm reaper, and other manufacturers produced much needed farm equipment that freed young farmers to fight in the war.

The end of the war did not spell the end of the industry boom in Chicago. George M. Pullman established the railroad sleeping car industry in 1867. The Union Pacific Railroad connected Chicago with San Francisco in 1869, and by 1870, there were some 300,000 residents in the city.

Abraham Lincoln was the 16th President of the United States.

The tempory City Hall in 1873, built after the Great Chicago Fire.

On the evening of October 8, 1871, the Great Chicago Fire began. Most historians believe that it started when a cow owned by Mrs. Patrick O'Leary kicked over a lighted lantern in her barn on DeKoven Street. Strong winds were blowing that night, and the flames spread. The fire raged for more than 24 hours, destroying 17,450 buildings and razing some three and one-third square miles of the city. The business district was wiped out, at least 300 people were killed, 90,000 were left homeless, and $200 million worth of property was lost.

But Chicago rose from the ashes as the people rebuilt. So well did they do the job that only 19 years later—in 1890—there were more than a million people living in the city, which by then was the second most populated city in the country, behind New York. In a way, tragic as it was, the fire might have been a good thing for the city. Many of the slums were burned down, and the opportunity to rebuild attracted many innovative architects. In addition, parks along the lake were laid out.

Industrial expansion did not bring prosperity to all. Labor unrest began in 1877, when the Michigan Central Railroad switchmen walked off the job on July 23, protesting that their already meager wages ($55 to $65 per month) were to be cut. On July 25, Chicago looked like a war zone: mobs of angry workers clashed with some 20,000 police and armed volunteers. There were battles on the Randolph Street

(Pages 30-31)
Chicago in flames during the Great Fire, as seen from the Randolph Street bridge.

The markets on South Water Street at the turn of the century.

Bridge and at the viaduct near Archer and Halsted streets. The strike was finally broken on July 26 by two companies of Regular Army troops, leaving 35 people dead.

On May 3, 1886, a riot occurred at the McCormick Harvester plant when six strikers were killed by police. The next day a mass meeting was called at the Haymarket, which was the block on Randolph Street between Desplaines and Halsted streets, and a crowd of about 1,500 gathered for the rally. After a number of fiery speeches calling for an end to police violence, policemen arrived at the scene to break up the crowd. Someone lobbed a bomb into the police ranks, and then shots were fired from both sides. The battle ended 15 minutes later. The Haymarket Riot claimed several lives, and more than 100 people were injured.

Jane Addams and Ellen Gates Starr founded Hull House on South Halsted Street in 1889. This was one

The Haymarket Riot was one of the bloodiest events in a period of great labor unrest.

A policeman and a detective raid an illegal still during Prohibition.

of the first settlement houses in the United States and was established to help immigrant factory workers who lived in the Chicago slums. Hull House became a center of social reform, and Addams worked tirelessly for improved working conditions. She turned her efforts to the cause of peace when the First World War broke out. In 1931, Addams won the Nobel Peace Prize.

Twenty-two years after the tragedy of the Chicago Fire, Chicago had recovered sufficiently to hold the World's Columbian Exposition. It was a world's fair, held in 1893, to celebrate the four-hundredth anniversary of the discovery of America by Christopher Columbus.

The 1920s and early 1930s comprised the Prohibition Era—that period when alcohol was banned in the United States. It was then that Chicago gained its reputation for crime and violence. In the 1920s alone there were over 500 gang murders.

Al Capone arrived in Chicago from New York in 1919, and by 1926 he was king of the rackets—especially the traffic in illegal alcohol. Soon his income was estimated to be some $70 million per year. The Chicago underworld gang wars reached their climax on St. Valentine's Day in 1929, when several gangsters, some of them disguised as policemen, shot down a rival group in the garage of the S.M.C. Cartage Company on North Clark Street. It wasn't until 1931 that Capone was sent to prison, convicted, of all things, for income tax evasion.

THREE CENTS

THE CHICAGO DAILY NEWS

54TH YEAR—39. COPYRIGHT 1929 BY THE CHICAGO DAILY NEWS INC. THURSDAY, FEBRUARY 14, 1929.—FORTY-EIGHT PAGES. FINAL EDITION

MASSACRE 7 OF MORAN G...

HAFFA CHANGES HIS MIND; WILL FIGHT PRISON

Owes It to Friends, He Says; Makes Bond, Prepares Appeal.

MAY STAY IN COUNCIL

After a night in the county jail, Ald. Titus Haffa of the 43d ward, free now on $25,000 bail, has changed his mind and decided he will fight against going to federal prison to serve a two-year sentence for bootlegging. He had announced yesterday that he would give up without a struggle and leave with a batch of prisoners scheduled to start for Leavenworth tomorrow night. Today he declared he'd go to the United States Supreme court if necessary to beat the "rap."

Haffa went free on bail this afternoon after Judge Walter C. Lindley had approved it at the federal building. The bond was put up by a security company. It assured Haffa's release for at least a few months while his appeal is being made.

Haffa, who refused in his changed attitude to say whether he would resign from the city council and withdraw from the aldermanic race, might have stuck out his chin defiantly as he made the announcement in the office of Warden Edward J. Fogarty, but he was deterred by a stiff neck which he blamed on conditions in the jail.

Changes His Mind.

Haffa's change of mind was made known after he had conferred for some time with his attorneys, Robert M. Woodward and Theodore Levin, both assistant state's attorneys under Crowe, and a friend, Edward Sklarov, precinct captain in Haffa's ward organization.

"Do I look like a crushed man?" the alderman, who was sentenced yesterday for conspiracy to violate the prohibition laws, challenged newspaper men. And he smiled his well-known smile, in sharp contrast to the appearance he presented as he was led from the federal building to the county jail.

"Maybe I did feel that way yesterday," he explained. "You know, I haven't any money and it takes a lot to perfect an appeal, but a lot of good friends have come to my aid. And since I'm innocent of this charge I believe I owe it to my friends and to my constituents not to go to the penitentiary without a vigorous fight in the Court of Appeals.

Joseph Bacheria and Edward Hug, the alderman's precinct captains, were each fined $3,000 and sentenced to serve one year and a day in the Leavenworth penitentiary. Sam Simons, reputed to have been Haffa's chief lieutenant in his liquor operations, was given a similar fine and ordered to the penitentiary for eighteen months.

Haffa found comfort yesterday in the thought that prohibition law violators are not viewed in the same light as other felons.

"If I do serve a sentence the people will not think I have done anything very wrong," he reflected. "If everybody who violated the law was in jail I guess most everybody would be there."

Denounced by Judge.

Haffa was severely denounced by Judge Lindley as he passed sentence.

"The evidence, if true, showed a grievous and horrible situation," the judge said. "Every public officer is a

[Continued on Fourth Page.]

WEATHER INDICATIONS.

[Feb. 14. 1929.]

Chicago and vicinity—Probably fair tonight and Friday, but some cloudiness; no decided change in temperature; lowest tonight 10 to 15 degrees above zero; winds mostly gentle to moderate westerly.

TWO OF VICTIMS AND SCENE OF LATEST GANGSTER OUTBREAK

STAYS GIVEN 2 OF 3 KILLERS DUE TO DIE TONIGHT

Shanks Faces the Electric Chair Alone; Seeks Sanity Test.

Due to die in the electric chair at midnight tonight, Charles Walz and Anthony Grecco, youthful police killers, got a temporary prolonged grip on life today when Judge Harry B. Miller granted them a stay of execution until next Wednesday to permit appeals to the Supreme court.

David Shanks, colored bootblack scheduled to die tonight with them, was having no such luck in last-minute appeals. Gov. Emmerson this afternoon refused again to grant a reprieve, and Shanks' last hope lay in the possibility of some judge's issuing a stay to allow a sanity test.

The state board of pardon and paroles likewise had turned him down in an emergency session held here this afternoon to determine whether he should be granted a sanity hearing.

Attorneys Assailed.

Judge Miller scored what he termed the lack of diligence on the part of Walz' and Grecco's attorneys in waiting until the eleventh hour to file their appeal.

"But the lack of diligence by these attorneys should not be used as punishment against the prisoners," the court added. "I believe these men are guilty and should be punished. But it seems that everything is put in the way of the law being vindicated. However, I am the last one to deprive a defendant of his rights. Therefore, since the attorneys say they will leave for Springfield at midnight tonight to file their appeal, I am going to grant a delay until next Wednesday to permit their petition to be considered."

Taken from Death Cell.

Walz, Grecco and Shanks had been lodged together in the death cell this

1929 FLAPPERS JUST EAT UP VALENTINES

Modern Greetings Take Line of Sandwich; Swains Spend $250,000 Here.

"I want a three-decker!" shouted a loop sheik as he bounced through the entrance to a State street store today.

"Yeh!" responded the clerk. "What'll it be—a sandwich or a valentine?"

The clerk explained his answer this way: The favorite model 1929 valentine is built like the popular sandwich, in three layers.

"That's the only kind the girl of today wants," he said. "You see, the three-decker has a lovely shaped heart for the top layer. How it thrills the lover's lady! Then the next two layers are appetizing bonbons, chocolates, wine-filled candies, dipped nuts and whatnot."

A tour of valentine counters in different stores revealed his judgment not to be far off. In large department stores the display of conventional valentines of old wouldn't surpass that of a cross-roads country store fifteen years ago. But the candy counters—they looked like Christmas was just around the corner!

Total expenditures throughout the city for valentines in all forms—cards, candy, flowers, etc.—were estimated by a store manager to be between $250,000 and $500,000.

Postmaster Arthur C. Lueder said that mail records indicate 1,000,000

Above—Crowd of curious persons attracted to "alky" distributing place at 2122 North Clark street today after north side gangsters were lined up against wall and slain by rival hoodlums. At right—Pete (above) and Frank Gusenberg, victims. Below—George (Bugs) Moran, leader of gang of which victims were members. Al Capone, head of gang blamed for wholesale killings.

[All pictures except those of the Gusenbergs by a staff photographer.]

Mind of World Is All on Romance, Will Finds

Special to The Chicago Daily News.

New York, Feb. 14.—Who cares about an inauguration? One of those every four years. Who cares whether we voted fifteen new cruisers or just a rowboat? The pope and Mussolini can't make the front page.

All those things are a lot of applesauce. The world's mind is on romance. It's Anne and Lindy that our minds are on today.

What do we care if Hoover catches a whale? Or Coolidge shoots a bear?

DECIDE TO CUT COOK ADRIFT IN TAX TANGLE

Solons to Rush Laws to Avert Downstate Tieup; Aid County Later.

BY WARREN PHINNEY.

Special Dispatch from a Staff Correspondent.

Springfield, Ill., Feb. 14.—Safety first for this year's tax collections by the state and all downstate counties and local taxing bodies is the policy just decided upon. Decision to cut the rest of the state free from Cook county's tax entanglements has been reached at a conference between Gov. Emmerson and a group of state officials, leaders of the legislature and Chicago tax experts.

Collection of all taxes downstate is endangered by the fixing of the state tax rate at 30 cents in advance of the completion of the Cook county reassessment. To ward off that peril, it is understood, Attorney-General Carlstrom is to prepare legislation which will be rushed through both houses.

The legislature and the state administration then are to do whatever they can to help Chicago out of its difficulties.

For one thing, Gov. Emmerson is expected to sign house bill No. 2, while the senate is to pass house bills 1 and 58, which already have passed the house. These three bills compose the remedial legislation sought with a hope of expediting completion of the 1928 reassessment in Cook county.

Matthews' Plans Introduced.

KILLING SCENE TOO GRUESOME FOR ONLOOKERS

View of Carnage Proves a Strain on Their Nerves.

IS LIKE A SHAMBLES

It's too much to tell. You go into the door marked "S-M-C Cartage company." You see a bunch of big men talking with restrained excitement in the cigarette smoke. You go through another door back of the front office. You go between two close-parked trucks in the garage.

Then you almost stumble over the head of the first man, with a clean gray felt hat still placed at the precise angle of gangster toughness.

The dull yellow light of a lamp in daytime shows dark rivulets of blood heading down to the drain that was meant for the water from washed cars. There are six of the red streams from six heads. The bodies—four of them well dressed in civilian clothes—two of them with their legs crossed as they wirled to fall.

It's too much, so you crowd on past the roadster with bullet holes in it to the big truck behind.

Too Much for the Dog.

You look at the truck. It is something to look at because the men were fixing it. It's jacked up, with one wheel off. You look and the big man called "Commissioner" looks and a crowd gathers, and then it gets too much for the police dog you had failed to notice lying under the truck, tied to it by a cheap yellow rope.

It gets too much for the big brown and gray police dog and he goes crazy. He barks, he howls, he snarls, showing wicked white teeth in bright red gums.

The crowd backs away. The dog yowls once more and subsides.

Your thoughts snap with a crack back to the circle of yellow lamplight, where six things that were men are sprawled.

It's still too much. You push out into the fresh air.

Quiet in Mid-Morning.

You find that traffic was quiet in front of 2122 North Clark street at 10:30 o'clock this morning. A streetcar rattled down the narrow way left by parked cars. Across from the high garage, two windows of one of those old-fashioned gray-stone apartment houses were open. Two women were exchanging gossip despite the cold.

A blue and black sedan stopped in front of the garage. The women exchanged their curiosities about it and then went back to gossip.

They jumped as a muffled roar reached them. The blue and black car sped away and turned the corner.

Out of nowhere the crowd came, pouring in from the rooming houses, the little stores, the automobiles, the street cars. They set up a hum. A policeman arrived—another. A police siren sounded—the clang of a patrol wagon.

The two women ran down and joined the buzzing in the street.

Gold Coast There, Too.

By this time people from the big apartment hotels on Lincoln Park West, half a block away, had heard and had come. The crowd was a cross section. Gold coast and Clark street merged in the gathering.

"What is it? Who were they? What did they do? Were they in the know? Double-crossers. Them guys had the pull and pulled it too strong——"

Inside six pairs of lips failed to answer.

U. S. Takes Hand in Killing of 7 Gangsters

The federal government, because of the bootleg evidence, took a hand in the investigation of the massacre of seven Moran gangsters today. John K. Northup, who tomorrow leaves the district attorney's office to join State's Attorney Swanson's staff, went

VICTIMS ARE LINED AGAINST WALL; ONE VOLLEY KILLS ALL

Assassins Pose as Policemen; Flee in "Squad Car" After Fusillade; Capone Revenge for Murder of Lombardo, Officers Believe.

Seven Moran-O'Banion gangsters were lined up against the wall of a beer-distributing point at 2122 North Clark street at 10:30 o'clock today. Four men, two of them in police uniforms, stood before them, armed with machine guns and sawed-off shot guns. The leader of the execution squad barked an order and the seven fell, six dying at once, the seventh three hours later.

The execution, carried out with the precision of a Mexican firing squad, is charged by the police to the Capone-Lombardo interests. Greatest in point of numbers, it was also the most cold-blooded in the history of Chicago's gangland slaughters.

The dead, as identified by the police, were:

GUSENBERG, PETER, notorious gunman for the O'Banion-Weiss-Drucci-Moran mob.

GUSENBERG, FRANK, brother of Peter. He died after the others were killed, but refused to talk, though conscious.

WEINSHANK, AL, north side "alky" peddler.

MAY, JOHN, 1249 West Madison street, a $50-a-week mechanic, apparently killed to silence him.

CLARK, JOHN, brother-in-law of George ("Bugs") Moran, leader of the gang.

DAVIS, ARTHUR, west side racketeer.

FOSTER, FRANK, hoodlum.

A second theory, advanced by federal prohibition agents, was that the massacre was perpetrated by a band of rum runners from Detroit and Ecorse to pay off the Moran gang for hi-jacking two truckloads of Chicago-bound Canadian whisky two weeks ago. This, the police agreed, would account for the boldness with which the killers operated.

Two other theories under consideration by the police are that the Moran gang and the Aiello clan, who have been working in harmony on the north side, may have fallen out with the Aiello gang, shooting first, and that today's slayings may have had some connection with the government conviction of Ald. Titus A. Haffa, in whose territory they operated. But little credence was given by the police to these theories.

The building at 2122 North Clark street, scene of the wholesale slaughter, is a one-story brick garage, its windows bearing the sign, "The S. M. C. Cartage company."

Scene Before Tragedy.

The scene, as reconstructed by a police racketeer expert, who viewed the shambles after the shooting was over, was about as follows:

This morning about 10 o'clock, as mail men heavily laden with the missives of St. Valentine's day went their rounds, seven men sat about the garage, two in the front, five others behind a wooden partition in the garage proper.

Four of the men were gathered about an electric stove on which bubbled a pot of coffee. A box of crackers and a half-dozen cups com-

[Continued on Third Page.]

War to Finish Russell's Plan

A hoodlum roundup unparalleled in Chicago's history—one that will far exceed the recent week-end wholesale arrests—was promised today by Police Commissioner William F. Russell the moment he looked upon the scene of the slaughter of six gangsters at 2122 North Clark street.

"It's war to the finish," the commissioner said. "I've never known of a challenge like this—the killers posing as policemen—but now that the challenge has been made it's accepted. We're going to make this the knell of gangdom in Chicago."

Immediately Commissioner Russell dispatched a runner to the city hall to send out a message on the police teletype to all detective squads and to order all available policemen organized to begin to "knock off" known hangouts of hoodlums.

"No matter how long it takes," Russell told his lieutenants, "I'm going to have my men working day and night for a week if necessary to clear up this situation. It's got to be done."

The police commissioner's words sounded the keynote for other officials who hurried to the scene.

Assistant State's Attorney David Stansbury took charge of the investigation for State's Attorney Swanson.

"I've heard of brutal gang killings in Chicago," he said, "but never anything quite equal to this. The gangsters by their very boldness have written their own doom."

Stansbury co-operated with Coroner Herman N. Bundesen, who was busy attempting to identify the victims and also supervising the removal of the bodies to undertaking rooms.

TODAY'S RACE RESULTS

AT MIAMI, FLA.

First—Sand Fiddler, 5-1; Billy Cook, 2-1; Texas Longhorn, 4-1.

Second—McIntosh, 6-1; La Vestale, 8-1; Loreen, 1-3.

Third—Black Bart, 4-1; Rosetta Stone, 8-5; Resourceful, out.

The St. Valentine's Day Massacre made front page news.

The year 1919 was also marked by racial violence. The 31st Street Beach on the South Side had always been segregated—part for whites, part for blacks—by mutual understanding. But in July, a 17-year-old black youth, holding onto a railroad tie, swam across the invisible line to the white side, and stones were thrown at him. The frightened young man let go of the tie and drowned. A fight ensued between blacks and whites on shore.

Al Capone leaving the courthouse during his trial for tax evasion.

For nearly a week Chicago was in a state of civil war. Blacks were mobbed, beaten, and stabbed. Whites were shot. Gangs took to the streets. Finally, the militia was called in. The confrontation left 36 people dead, 537 people injured, and 1,000 homeless.

It was during this period that Chicago Jazz was born. Right after World War I ended, great New Orleans jazz musicians, such as "King" Joe Oliver, Sidney Bechet, Kid Ory, and Louis Armstrong, began arriving in Chicago. They were met by a group of Chicago high school boys who had been playing jazz for fun—such musicians as Benny Goodman (clarinet), Bud Freeman (saxophone), George Wettling (drums), Gene Krupa (drums), Frank Teschemacher (clarinet), Jimmy McPartland (cornet), Dave Tough (drums), Art Hodes (piano), Muggsy Spanier (cornet), Eddie Condon (guitar), and Bix Beiderbecke (cornet and piano). Out of this meld came a new art form— "Chicago Jazz." Chicago style was based on New Orleans blues, but it was frenzied and intense. And it was the Chicago style that was to endure.

In 1933 and 1934, Chicago celebrated its hundredth birthday with a world's fair—"A Century of Progress." It was erected on filled-in land near the present Miegs Field on Lake Michigan. The fair included a Hall of Science that featured an atomic energy exhibit— something almost unheard of at the time. It also had a Sky Ride—a terrifying trip high over the fair. The Travel and Transportation Building had a modern

Benny Goodman playing clarinet with his band, during the era when jazz and swing music filled Chicago's nightclubs.

suspended roof, and the Owens Illinois House started the 1930s fad for glass-block construction.

Despite the tremendous changes in the first third of the twentieth century, many workers felt that their lives had changed little for the better. On May 30, 1937, strikers from the Republic Steel plant on the South Side were coming out of a peaceful meeting, and about 300 of them began to walk toward the plant entrance, where the police were waiting for them. The police opened fire, leaving 10 people dead

The Carillion Tower rises out of the Hall of Science at the 1933 Chicago World's Fair, which was the city's way of celebrating its hundredth birthday.

Full view of the Hall of Science, which featured an atomic energy exhibit and a Sky Ride.

and 90 wounded in the first 30 seconds. Still not satisfied, the police chased the fleeing crowd and knocked down and beat 28 more. The strike came to a sudden end.

The outbreak of World War II in 1941 brought a massive infusion of money for war plants—$1.3 billion in Chicago alone. Undoubtedly, the city's most important contribution to the war happened under the stands of Stagg Field—the stadium where the University of Chicago played its football games. On December 2, 1942, the first controlled atomic reaction was set off under the direction of Enrico Fermi (who had won the Nobel Prize in physics in 1938). Fermi and his team of scientists laid the groundwork not only for the atomic bomb that won the war but also for the nuclear industry as we know it.

It is hard, now, to imagine the scale of new construction that took place in the 1950s and 1960s. Chicago's first subway opened in 1956, and the Eisenhower Expressway was completed in 1959. With the opening of the St. Lawrence Seaway in 1959, Chicago classified as a world port, since large sea-going vessels could now sail from the Atlantic Ocean to the city and back. To celebrate the event, the city hosted the International Trade Fair, an event so important that Queen Elizabeth II of Great Britain paid a visit.

Urban renewal in the fifties and sixties cleared some 800 acres of slums to make room for new low-cost housing. Between 1958 and 1963, more than 25 new buildings were completed or were under construction in the downtown section. More expressways were built in the early 1960s, ringing the city.

Since then, two huge water filtration plants, the McCormick Place Convention and Exposition Center, O'Hare Airport, and the Richard J. Daley Civic Center have been built. Magnificent commercial, as well as apartment, buildings were built in the downtown area and along the North Side lakefront: the John Hancock Center (1127 feet, 100 stories), the First National Bank Building (852 feet, 60 stories), the Sears Tower (the world's tallest building—1454 feet, 110 stories), the Amoco Building (1136 feet, 80 stories), and the

Water Tower Place (the world's tallest reinforced concrete building—859 feet, 74 stories).

Today, Chicago is really "The City That Works." O'Hare International Airport is the world's busiest, with some 65,000 takeoffs and landings per year. More than 500 truck and bus lines are based in Chicago, and it is the world's greatest railway center. It is also the leading wholesale distributing center, with its Chicago Board of Trade, where 90 percent of the country's contracts for delivery of grains are made; its Chicago Mercantile Exchange, which is the busiest market for farm products; and its preponderance of large mail-order houses.

Chicago's past has certainly been "stormy, husky, brawling," as Sandburg wrote. But it also exemplifies the pride and tenacity of a diverse people struggling to make a life, and a city, worthy of their best hopes for the future.

(*At left*)
Interior of the Chicago Board of Trade.

THE
PEOPLE

"... it is a city of cities—made of
great foreign blocs of population
impinging on one another.
The Polish settlement here, next to
Warsaw, is the largest Polish
city in the world. There is also
a sizeable German city, and a
big Czech city, and an Italian town,
and a Jewish city, and a
Scandinavian borough that stretches
for miles, and an Irish town."

Albert Halper—American author

Chicago's outdoor plazas are perfect places for residents
and visitors alike to enjoy the city's beauty.

44

During the latter half of the nineteenth century, Europeans came to the United States in droves. The first to arrive in Chicago were the Germans and the Irish. Later came the Italians, Poles, Hungarians, and Lithuanians. They settled in their own neighborhoods, often retaining much of their old culture and customs. Still later came the blacks, Hispanics, and Orientals. After World War II, displaced persons from Europe began to arrive, followed by displaced Asians, Latin Americans, Russian Jews, and Assyrian Chinese.

Chicago is the largest Polish city in the world, after Warsaw. It is the third largest Greek city and the fourth largest Croatian city. There are still many ethnic neighborhoods left, and in them one can hear dozens of different languages and eat the food of some 50 foreign countries. There is an Old Greek Town and a New Greek Town (centered at the intersection of Western, Lincoln, and Lawrence avenues), Italian neighborhoods near the University of Illinois Chicago campus, Mexicans in the Pilsen District (around Ashland Avenue and West 18th Street), Scandinavians in Andersonville (Clark Street between Lawrence and Foster avenues), and Irish in Bridgeport (just south of Chinatown).

Chicago has produced more than its fair share of famous or influential people. For example, it has always been a haven for writers of all sorts. The roll call of writers who called Chicago home is

Students relax on the campus of the University of Illinois at Chicago.

impressive—Saul Bellow, Studs Terkel, Carl Sandburg, Nelson Algren, Theodore Dreiser, Edna Ferber, Sherwood Anderson, Thornton Wilder, and Richard Wright come to mind. And many famous writers were born in the city, such as Edgar Rice Burroughs (creator of Tarzan) and Raymond Chandler (creator of Philip Marlowe). Other Chicago natives are James Gould Cozzens (*By Love Possessed*), Michael Crichton (*The Andromeda Strain*), John Dos Passos (*U.S.A.*), James T. Farrell (*The Young Manhood of Studs Lonigan*), Lorraine Hansberry (*A Raisin in the Sun*), Alison Lurie (*The War Between the Tates*), David Mamet (*Glengarry Glen Ross*), and Shel Silverstein (*Where the Sidewalk Ends*).

Lorraine Hansberry is the author of *Raisin In the Sun,* the first play by a black woman produced on Broadway.

Chicago has had a long history of excellent journalism, although the Chicago style occasionally possessed a large number of quirks. These quirks are probably best exemplified by the play, *The Front Page,* written by two veteran Chicago newspapermen, Charles MacArthur and Ben Hecht. The play has been made into a movie on several occasions and tells the hilarious story of newsroom feuds and underhanded manipulations by editors and reporters. Many native Chicagoans have made significant contributions to journalism, such as John Chancellor, John Gunther, Hugh Hefner, Mike Royko, Gene Siskel, Herbert Block (Herblock), and William S. Paley.

Music has been a part of the Chicago scene for generations. The Chicago Symphony Orchestra is

(At left)
The Sears Tower rises above a skyline that bears the imprint of some of the world's great architects.

hailed by many critics as the best in the world. The city gave birth to many jazz legends—Benny Goodman, Gene Krupa, Ramsey Lewis, Jimmy McPartland, Muggsy Spanier, and Mel Torme, to name but a few. In pop music, Quincy Jones, Frankie Laine, and Anita O'Day are Chicagoans. And in the soul-rock-rhythm and blues area, so were Sam Cooke, Lou Rawls, Minnie Riperton, Grace Slick, and Patti Smith.

Chicago loves comedy. One of the finest—and oldest—comedy clubs in the nation is Second City, and it has given the nation many of its most famous comics. Native-born Chicagoans who have made people laugh are John Belushi, Edgar Bergen, Shelly Berman, and Harvey Korman.

Chicago's first African American mayor, Harold Washington, was elected in 1983.

Although born in New York, Studs Terkel is a colorful journalist closely associated with Chicago.

Chicago, an early pioneer in movies and television, has supplied the entertainment world with many personalities. Among them are Ralph Bellamy, Jim Belushi, Tempestt Bledsoe, Tom Bosley, Bruce Dern, Walt Disney, Harrison Ford, Marla Gibbs, Michael Gross, Daryl Hannah, Marilu Henner, Richard Kiley, Donald O'Connor, Jason Robards, Jr., Pat Sajak, David Soul, Mr. T, Raquel Welch, George Wendt, Robin Williams, and Robert Young.

ON THE TOUR BUS

As far as places to visit, things to see, and education to be gained, some cities are worth a day or two, some a month or two, but Chicago is worth a lifetime. It is a city in which the arts flourish. Many of its museums are unrivaled. Its universities are world famous. And its sports fans are among the most knowledgeable in the country. Here are some of the places and things that delight both natives and visitors.

The Loop

Landmarks and Buildings

The *Richard J. Daley Center and Plaza* at Randolph and Clark streets (649 feet, 31 stories) is the home of both county and city courts, plus administrative offices. One of the most famous department stores in the world is *Marshall Field's* on North State Street. The clock outside the building projects over the sidewalk, and generations of Chicagoans have met friends "under the clock." Inside the building are a 14-story-high inner court and a six-story rotunda with a Tiffany Dome of some 1,600,000 separate pieces of glass. *Carson Pirie Scott & Company*, at State and Madison streets, is another famous Chicago department store. The architect for the building was the great Louis Sullivan, and the building is a

Marshall Field's Department Store occupies an entire block in the Loop.

The Chicago Board of Trade.

historic landmark. The *Chicago Public Library Cultural Center*, on East Washington Street, is also a historic landmark, with Tiffany glass domes, mosaics, and marble walls and stairs. Programs are held and exhibits are on display here. *Orchestra Hall*, on South Michigan Avenue, was built in 1904 and is the home of the Chicago Symphony Orchestra.

The *Auditorium Building*, built in 1889 and designed by Louis Sullivan and Dankmar Adler, is also on South Michigan Avenue. The *Monadnoch Building*, on West Jackson Boulevard, one of the oldest skyscrapers in town, was constructed between 1889 and 1893. At the time, it was the tallest and largest office building in the world. *The Rookery*, on South LaSalle Street, was built in 1886 and is the oldest remaining steel-skeleton skyscraper in the world. Built in 1929, the *Chicago Board of Trade*, on West Jackson Boulevard, is the largest commodity futures exchange in the world. The *Sears Tower* (1,454 feet, 110 stories), on South Wacker Drive, is the tallest building in the world. The *Civic Opera Building*, on North Wacker Drive, was built in 1929 and houses not only the 3,600-seat *Civic Opera House* and the 900-seat *Civic Theatre*, but also contains 45 floors of commercial office space. The *Chicago Mercantile Exchange*, built in 1983 on South Wacker Drive, is the world's leading financial futures and options exchange. Built in 1933, the United States *Post Office* on West Van Buren Street is the largest post office under one roof in the world.

Museums

The *Spertus Museum of Judaica*, on South Michigan Avenue, contains Hebraic art objects and many other ethnic materials from ancient to modern times. Located at Michigan Avenue and Adams Street, the *Art Institute of Chicago*, erected in 1879, is world famous for its collection of American and European art. On West Randolph Street, the *Telephony Museum* displays early telephone equipment, including the original cabinet telephone used by Alexander Graham Bell in 1892.

Enjoying Spring outside the Art Institute of Chicago.

Churches

The *Chicago Temple*, on West Washington Street, is a Methodist Church and has the highest church spire in the world (568 feet).

Outdoor Art and Plazas

The *Batcolumn*, erected in 1976, is located on West Madison Street, and is a 100-foot tall, 20-ton welded steel sculpture in the shape of a baseball bat by Claes Oldenburg. The *Picasso sculpture*, at Wash-

The Picasso sculpture was a gift to the city from the artist.

ington and Dearborn streets, is an abstract 50-foot tall, 162-ton creation of Pablo Picasso. The *Miró sculpture*, also at Washington and Dearborn, is an abstract sculpture created by Joan Miró that is 35 feet tall. At Monroe and Dearborn streets is the *Chagall mosaic*, a 3000-square foot work of abstract mosaic art called "The Four Seasons," by Marc Chagall. The *Calder stabile*, called "Flamingo," at Adams and Dearborn streets, is an Alexander Calder abstract sculpture that is 53 feet high and weighs 50 tons. Erected in 1975, the *Bertoia sculpture*, by Harry Bertoia, is located on East Randolph Street and is set in a reflecting pool.

Parks and Zoos

Grant Park stretches from Randolph Street to McFetridge Drive along Lake Michigan and contains the beautiful *Buckingham Fountain* and its nearby formal gardens.

North Side

Landmarks and Buildings

Navy Pier, at the east end of Grand Avenue, extends almost one mile into Lake Michigan. Its East Promenade has an auditorium, park benches, old streetlights, and landscaping, and affords many spectacular views of the Chicago skyline. At

Buckingham Fountain has a spectacular light and water display on summer nights.

the foot of Ohio Street is the *Clipper*, a restored 1905 Great Lakes passenger steamer that can be toured. The *John Hancock Center* (1127 feet, 100 stories), on North Michigan Avenue, is the world's tallest office/residential skyscraper. There is an observatory at the top. Also on North Michigan Avenue is the *Water Tower Place*; it contains more than 125 shops, 11 restaurants, 7 movie theaters, and the Ritz-Carlton Hotel. The *Water Tower*, at Chicago and Michigan avenues, was built in 1869 and is a fortlike structure that survived the Chicago Fire. *Tribune Tower*, the home of the *Chicago Tribune*, on North Michigan Avenue, is an oddity—a Gothic-style skyscraper. Another skyscraper on North Michigan Avenue is the Wrigley Building. This blindingly white structure was built in two sections, connected by a bridge on the third

Water Tower Place. Practically a city within itself.

floor. The *Sun-Times Building*, home of the *Chicago Sun-Times*, is on North Wabash Avenue and contains one of the most modern newspaper plants in the country. Built in 1963, *Marina City*, on North State Street, includes two 550-feet circular buildings, a marina, and boat storage. At Wells Street and the Chicago River is the *Merchandise Mart* (built in 1930), one of the world's largest commercial buildings. The *Newberry Library* on West Walton Street was built in 1887 and has many internationally famous collections.

Museums

The *Museum of Contemporary Art* specializes in modern paintings and sculpture and is located on East Ontario Street. On Michigan Avenue, the *Terra Museum of American Art* has a splendid collection of works by American artists of the eighteenth, nineteenth, and twentieth centuries. The *Peace Museum*, on West Erie Street, has displays of art, science, labor, women, religious institutions, and minorities as regards their roles in the search for peace. On North Lake Shore Drive is the *International Museum of Surgical Sciences*, which contains a large collection of ancient surgical instruments, plus paintings and exhibits on the

The Marina City Apartments rise like corn cobs from their base.

history of surgery. The *Chicago Historical Society*, at Clark Street and North Avenue, has a magnificent collection of objects illustrating the history of the city. On North Clark Street, in a building erected in 1857, is the *Chicago Academy of Sciences*, with its natural history and wildlife displays. The *Polish Museum of America*, on Milwaukee Avenue, has exhibits of Polish culture, folklore, and art.

Churches

The *Fourth Presbyterian Church*, at Michigan Avenue and Delaware Place, was built in the

Inside the Field Museum of Natural History.

Gothic style in 1914. On North State Street is the *Roman Catholic Holy Name Cathedral*, a Neo-Gothic church completely renovated in 1969. The *Moody Church* on North Clark Street contains a 4000-seat auditorium and a 4400-pipe organ.

Parks and Zoos

The largest park in the city is *Lincoln Park*, which is located along the lake and stretches almost the entire length of the North Side. It contains beaches, biking and jogging paths, many statues, and a golf course, as well as a zoo and a conservatory. The *Lincoln Park Zoological Gardens* has more than 2200 animals and includes a farm and a children's zoo. The *Lincoln Park Conservatory* boasts four glassed buildings and formal and rock gardens.

South Side

Landmarks and Buildings

McCormick Place-On-The-Lake, on South Lake Shore Drive, is a huge, self-contained exposition and meeting complex. Designed by Frank Lloyd Wright, *Robie House*, on South Woodlawn Avenue, was one of this great architect's first buildings. The *Prairie Avenue Historic District*, between 18th and Cullerton streets, is the area where Chicago's millionaires lived during the 1880s. It contains cobblestone streets, gaslights, the *Clarke House* (1836), the *Glessner House* (1886), *Kimball House* (1890), *Coleman House* (1886), and *Keith House* (1871).

Museums

The *Adler Planetarium*, on South Lake Shore Drive, has

A sculpture by Henry Moore outside the Adler Planetarium.

astronomical exhibits as well as sky shows. Also to be found on South Lake Shore Drive is the John G. Shedd Aquarium, where more than 8000 aquatic animals of more than 800 species are on display. The *Field Museum of Natural History*, at Roosevelt Road and Lake Shore Drive, is one of the largest natural history museums in the world. The *Museum of Science and Industry*, on South Lake Shore Drive at 57th Street, is arguably the best science museum in the world and has many hands-on exhibits. The *Oriental Institute Museum*, on East 58th Street on the campus of the University of Chicago, contains an outstanding collection of artifacts from the Near East. Located on East Hyde Park Boulevard is the *Morton B. Weiss Museum of Judaica*, with its collections of rare manuscripts and Iranian Judaica artifacts. The *Du Sable Museum of African-American History*, on East 56th Place, has a collection of African-American art objects and displays on black history. On South Pulaski Road is the *Balzekas Museum of Lithuanian Culture*, which contains Lithuanian artifacts and memorabilia collections and a children's museum.

Churches
The *Rockefeller Memorial Chapel*, on the campus of the University of Chicago at South Woodlawn Avenue, is a Gothic building with a 72-bell carillon.

The Museum of Science and Industry is located in Jackson Park.

West Side
Landmarks and Buildings
Hull House, on South Halsted Street, was founded by Nobel Peace Prize winner Jane Addams and Ellen Gates Starr, and contains the Hull Mansion (1856) and the dining hall (1905).

Museums
The *Chicago Fire Academy*, on West DeKoven Street, is built on the site where it is believed that the Chicago Fire started. Here one can take a tour of the facilities used for training firefighters. On West Washington Boulevard is the *Museum of Holography*, with its extensive collections of holograms.

Churches
Our Lady of Sorrows Basilica, on West Jackson Boulevard, was built between 1890 and 1902.

Parks and Zoos
Garfield Park and Conservatory, on North Central Park Boulevard, has outdoor formal

gardens and eight greenhouses. Although it is not in the city proper, but rather in the suburb of Brookfield, the Brookfield Zoo is also called the Chicago Zoological Park. One of the finest zoos in the world, it contains barless enclosures, three indoor rain forests, dolphin shows, safari tours, and a children's zoo.

Classical Music

Orchestra Hall is the home of not only the Chicago Symphony Orchestra, but also the Chicago

The arts have long held a prominent place in the city's culture.

Wrigley Field is home to the Chicago Cubs.

Civic Orchestra. Opera performances are given by both the Lyric Opera of Chicago and the Civic Opera at the *Civic Opera Building*. During the summer, the Grant Park Symphony gives concerts in *Grant Park's James C. Petrillo Music Shell*, on the corner of Jackson Boulevard and Columbus Drive.

Professional Sports

In baseball, the Chicago Cubs, of the National League, play in *Wrigley Field*, at North Clark and Addison streets; the Chicago White Sox, of the American League, play in *Comiskey Park*, at South Shields Avenue and 35th Street. The Chicago Bears, of the National Football League, play in *Soldier Field*, at Lake Shore Drive and East McFetridge Drive. The Chicago Bulls, of the National Basketball Association, and the Chicago Black Hawks, of the National Hockey League, share the *Chicago Stadium* on West Madison Street.

Universities

There are too many universities in the city to list all of them, but here are the more prominent.

In the Loop

Roosevelt University was founded in 1945, and has some 6000 students.

On the North Side

Northwestern University's Chicago Campus was established in 1920, and has 5084 students. DePaul University, founded in 1898, has 15,387 students, and has two campuses. Loyola University also has two campuses, was founded in 1870, and has an enrollment of 14,252.

On the South Side

The University of Chicago, founded in 1891, has 7800 students. Illinois Institute of Technology was founded in 1892, and has 6000 students.

On the West Side

The University of Illinois at Chicago was founded in 1965, and has an enrollment of 25,000.

Annual Events

The *Chicago Auto Show* is held on the second weekend in February at McCormick Place. The *St. Patrick's Day Parade* is held on March 17, and the Chicago River is dyed green for the occasion. Navy Pier is the home for the *Chicago International Art Exposition*, which is held in mid-May. *Taste of Chicago*, featuring samples of food provided by many Chicago restaurants, is held in Grant Park in the summer (the dates vary from year to year). The Grant Park *July 4 Concert* features cannons accompanying the Grant Park Symphony playing Tchaikovsky's *1812 Overture*. The *Air and Water Show* at Chicago Avenue at the lake features the Blue Angels precision flying team and the Golden Knights parachute team, and is held in mid-July. On the third weekend in July, the annual *Chicago to Mackinac Race* is held, in which many yachts participate. The *Gold Coast Art Fair* is held in August. The *Venetian Night Festival* in late August features a parade of illuminated yachts. The *Chicago Jazz Festival* is held in early September. The *Chicago International Film Festival* is celebrated throughout the city during two weeks in late October.

The Chicago Bears on the field with the New York Jets.

A player from the Chicago White Sox signing autographs.

CHRONOLOGY

1673	Marquette and Joliet discover the Chicago portage.	1871	The Great Chicago Fire destroys much of the city.
1779	Du Sable opens his trading post.	1884	The world's first skyscraper is built in Chicago.
1794	Chicago is ceded by the native Americans to the United States.	1886	Several are killed in the Haymarket Riot.
1803	The first Fort Dearborn is built.	1893	Chicago holds its first world's fair.
1812	Native Americans massacre the soldiers and settlers and burn the fort.	1919	Al Capone arrives in town.
		1929	The St. Valentine's Day Massacre occurs.
1816	Fort Dearborn is rebuilt.	1933	Chicago begins its second world's fair.
1830	Chicago's boundaries are laid out.	1942	The first controlled atomic reaction is set off in Chicago.
1833	Chicago is incorporated as a town.		
1837	Chicago is incorporated as a city.	1955	Richard J. Daley is elected mayor. O'Hare International Airport opens.
1848	The Illinois and Michigan Canal is completed.	1956	The Chicago subway begins service.
1848	The Galena and Chicago Union Railroad begins service.	1959	Chicago's first automobile expressway is opened. The St. Lawrence Seaway is opened, and Chicago holds an International Trade Fair.
1860	Abraham Lincoln is nominated for president in Chicago.		
1865	The Union Stockyards are opened.	1965	University of Illinois at Chicago opens.
1867	The Pullman railroad sleeping car factory is opened.	1968	Race riots erupt after the assassination of Dr. Martin Luther King, Jr. Demonstrations disrupt the Democratic convention.
1869	The Union Pacific Railroad links Chicago with San Francisco.		

1969	The "Chicago Seven" are indicted for violating the antiriot clause of the Civil Rights Act during the Democratic convention. They are found not guilty.	1975	Mayor Daley dies.
		1979	Jane Byrne is the first woman to be elected mayor of Chicago.
1971	The Union Stockyards are closed.	1983	Harold Washington becomes the city's first black mayor.
		1987	Mayor Washington dies.
1974	The Sears Tower is built. It is the world's tallest building.	1989	Richard M. Daley is elected mayor.

For Further Reading

Algren, Nelson. *Chicago: City on the Make*. Doubleday & Company, 1951.

Asbury, Herbert. *Gem of the Prairie*. Alfred A. Knopf, 1940.

Aylesworth, Thomas G. and Virginia L. *Chicago*. Bison Books, 1985.

Aylesworth, Thomas G. and Virginia L. *Chicago: The Glamour Years*. Gallery Books, 1986.

Bach, Ira J. *Chicago's Famous Buildings: A Photographic Guide to the City's Architectural Landmarks and Other Notable Buildings*. 3rd ed. University of Chicago Press, 1980.

Cromie, Robert. *A Short History of Chicago*. Lexikos, 1984.

Cutler, Irving. *Chicago: Metropolis of the Mid-Continent*. 3rd ed. Kendall/Hunt, 1982.

Fodor's Chicago. McKay, 1989.

Grossman, Ron. *Guide to Chicago Neighborhoods*. New Century Publishers, 1981.

Lieberman, Archie, and Robert Cromie. *Chicago in Color*. Hastings House Publishers, 1969.

Longstreet, Stephen. *Chicago*. McKay, 1973.

Masters, Edgar Lee. *The Tale of Chicago*. G. P. Putnam's Sons, 1933.

Terkel, Studs. *Chicago*. Pantheon, 1986.

Wagenknecht, Edward. *Chicago*. University of Oklahoma Press, 1964.

Where to Get More Information

The Association of Commerce and Industry
200 North LaSalle Street
Chicago, Illinois 60601

INDEX